THIS BOOK
BELONGS TO:

"DEAR PAINTERS,

EVERY DASH OF COLOR YOU BRING TO LIFE ON THE PAGES OF THIS BOOK IS A JOURNEY OF SERENITY AND CARE FOR OUR PRECIOUS OCEAN AND ITS INHABITANTS, THE SEA TURTLES. EACH BRUSHSTROKE IS A GESTURE OF LOVE AND RESPECT FOR THESE INCREDIBLE CREATURES THAT GLIDE GRACEFULLY BENEATH THE WAVES.

AS YOU COLOR, REMEMBER THE IMPORTANCE OF PROTECTING OUR VAST MARINE WORLD. EVERY DETAIL THEY FILL WITH COLOR IS A GENTLE REMINDER THAT WE ARE THE CARETAKERS OF THESE FRAGILE ECOSYSTEMS AND THE LIVES THAT INHABIT THEM.

JUST AS TURTLES SWIM CALMLY AND WISELY IN THEIR SEAS, MAY YOUR HANDS GUIDE THE BRUSHES WITH THE SAME DELICACY AND RESPECT. MAY THIS COLORING EXPERIENCE BE AN OPPORTUNITY NOT ONLY TO EXPRESS YOUR CREATIVITY, BUT ALSO TO NURTURE YOUR CONNECTION WITH OUR PLANET AND ITS AQUATIC WONDERS.

ALWAYS REMEMBER THAT JUST AS A DROP OF WATER CONTRIBUTES TO THE OCEAN, EVERY ACTION WE TAKE TO PROTECT OUR MARINE ENVIRONMENT MAKES A DIFFERENCE. MAY THE SERENITY WE FIND IN THIS BOOK INSPIRE US TO CARE FOR AND PRESERVE THE OCEAN AND ITS CREATURES FOR FUTURE GENERATIONS.

WITH GRATITUDE AND SERENITY,
[CLAUDIA ABATI]"